AUTHENTICALLY
HIS

AUTHENTICALLY
HIS

*28 Devotionals
for Christian Teens*

———

JIM WILLIAMS

———

Beacon Hill Press of Kansas City
Kansas City, Missouri

To
my wife, Cindi,
and my children, Sean and Sara.
It is my ultimate desire
to demonstrate to you daily
what it means to become
authentically His.

Preface

I'm on a journey, and I invite you to join me.

I want you to join me on a journey to rediscovering what it means to be authentic. The journey began for me many years ago when I asked Jesus into my heart. Since that time I have tried to discover what it means to become authentic—what it means to live an authentic, consistent life in an imitation world.

I've discovered a few things as I've traveled the narrow road. Perhaps you have too.

1. I've discovered that Christianity is a supernatural walk with a living, dynamic, personal, speaking God.
2. I've discovered that my relationships are on two levels. The first is my vertical relationship with God; the second is my horizontal relationship with others.
3. I've discovered that my relationship with others is dependent upon my relationship with God. If my relationship with God is growing, dynamic, and intimate, my relationship with my family and my friends will be growing and dynamic as well. Yet if my relationship with God is cold and stagnant, my relationship with others . . . well, you know what I mean!

There is a clarion call today for young people to become authentic, to take off your masks and become all God has dreamed you can become.

In a world where inconsistency is the norm, God is calling young people to go against the flow—to stem the tide that is eroding the character and commitment of a new generation. God's call to you is to be *authentically His*—to be the real deal—not only to talk the talk but to walk the walk.

The purpose of this devotional book is to help you identify areas in your life that God wants to change and to allow you to become who you are in Christ. For the next 28 days, let's stand before the mirror and reflect consistency in what we say and do. As a matter of fact, in writing to a teenager named Timothy, Paul said something like this: *Don't let others set an unauthentic example . . . but you set an authentic example in speech, love, life, faith and purity* (1 Tim. 4:12).

Are you ready to join me in the journey? Let's begin!

Tips for Using This Book

Here are a few tips that will assist you in getting the most out of this devotional book.

Commit a time—Select the best time of the day for you, when there would be approximately 15 to 20 minutes of uninterrupted time to work through the devotional exercise.

Commit a place—Pick a place in your home that will become your special place to meet God in the next 28 days. Discipline yourself to use the same place each day.

Begin with prayer—Start your time with God with a word of praise and a request for understanding of what He wants to say to you through the Word and the devotional.

Use your Bible—Each day a passage of Scripture is to be read from your own Bible before you read the devotional thought for the day. Some are brief; some include entire chapters. Read just one devotional a day, and place a checkmark on the page after you are done to note your progress.

Memorize Scripture—I challenge you to memorize the scripture highlighted at the end of the devotional. It is the verse(s) for the day or verse(s) from a larger passage of Scripture that has (have) been selected. Your spiritual life will be strengthened through the memorizing of God's Word.

Reflect—Think back on what you have read and have begun memorizing. Space has been provided at the bottom of each page for you to write out either the scripture you are memorizing or a brief thought that comes to mind. Think about what God is teaching you throughout your day. Meditate upon Him anytime, anyplace.

Respond—Take specific action in response to what God is teaching you. Put the Word into practice.

Develop a prayer partnership—While time spent alone with God is vital, the support and accountability found with a prayer partner is a great encouragement to follow through with commitments you made or to share insights gained. Challenge a friend to join you in these 28 days—and beyond! You may want to start a small prayer group in your home or at school.

Honest to God?

READ: Rom. 12:1-2

I remember the slogans of my childhood days. Some of them are still around today, but most of them are long gone. For example, if you were making a promise to someone, and that person wanted to really seal the promise, he or she would ask you: "Cross your heart and hope to die?" Immediately you would answer, "Cross my heart and hope to die" at the same time as you were crossing your heart with your hand. But if you didn't really mean it, you would put your other hand behind your back and cross your fingers, because most promises weren't deserving of death.

Another phrase we would throw around was "Honest injun!" But I guess the phrase we used when we really wanted to make sure someone was really telling the truth was "honest to God"—which meant "As God is my witness, I'm telling the truth."

Through my years of walking with God, I have discovered a brand-new meaning to the phrase "honest to God." I've learned that many times we as Christians don't like to stand in front of the mirror and really become honest with God. When we fail to become honest, there is an inconsistency that becomes commonplace between our talk and our walk. Too often we live one way when the spotlight is on us and another way when we're behind the four walls of our private world.

If we are to become transparent and authentic, there must be a consistency between our words and our actions and between our claimed values and our actual priorities. If something is authentic, it must conform to what it represents or claims to be.

I believe the greatest challenge facing Christian teens today is the very thing that is eating away at their character and integrity—unauthentic Christianity.

There is a call to come back to authentic Christian living—to conform to that which we represent. I challenge you today to stand in front of the mirror and take a good look at who you are.

Does your walk match your talk? If it does, you're well on your way to becoming *authentically His*—honest to God!

Memorize: Rom. 12:1-2

Prayer: Jesus, during these next few weeks, help me to stand in front of the mirror and understand what it means to be honest about my relationship with You.

The Key to Authenticity TUESDAY • **2**

READ: Ps. 46:10

During my 35 years of living I've heard many definitions of what Christianity means. The best one I've ever heard comes from Bill Hybels. He said—

Christianity is a supernatural walk with a living, dynamic, speaking, personal God.*

I like that, don't you? If I want to become authentically His, then I must understand that authentic Christianity begins with spiritual authenticity. Spiritual authenticity is a vital *daily* relationship with a real, personal, intimate God.

To recognize this is just the beginning of a supernatural walk. An authentic relationship with Jesus Christ takes time—not throwaway or leftover time, but *priority time* and *quality time*.

Our schedules are so crowded as it is—who has that kind of time to spend with God? We get so caught up in the pace of our lives that when we do try to spend time with God, it's usually so late at night that we fall asleep while the Word rests on our chests. We think that somehow by osmosis we will receive something from God. That's a far cry from spiritual authenticity.

If we want to thrive in our fast-paced society, we have to keep moving. We rev our engines to 20,000 rpms and we keep them revved 24 hours a day. If you can relate, don't hurry past my next statement: We rev our engines soooo fast that we zoom past the God we love and serve.

The pace—the speed—the fast track! When do we hear the still, small voice of God? When do we slow down to meet Him? When do we slow down to seek wisdom and direction? When do we enjoy a life-changing conversation with God? Not often? Sometimes? Never?

To build spiritual authenticity into our lives, we have to declare war on the things that rob us of quality time and separate us from the God we love. To become *authentically His*, we must declare war against whatever worldly entanglements keep us from spending quality time with God every day. We have to set new agendas with godly values. I hope you hear the clear call to *slow down*. Be still and know that *He is God.*

Memorize: Ps. 46:10

Prayer: Jesus, help me to slow down—slow down long enough to hear Your voice and to respond in radical obedience.

*Bill Hybels, *Honest to God* (Grand Rapids: Zondervan Publishing House, 1990), 13.

Achan Breakin' Heart—
The Cycle of Sin

READ: Josh. 7:20-21

It was an incredible victory!—perhaps the greatest victory the army of Israel had ever won. They had just gone up against a powerhouse called Jericho and defeated them soundly. The celebration was immense, and everyone came around Joshua, congratulating him on the greatest victory of his career.

The next assignment was to go to a place called Ai and assess how many men were needed to demolish this small city. Thinking this was going to be a cake walk, Joshua sent about 3,000 men, and—wouldn't you know it?—the men of Ai routed the army of Israel.

Joshua was heartbroken! Actually he was so hurt he tore off his clothes (I wouldn't advise you to do this!) and began to talk to the Lord. The Lord said there was sin in the camp. Israel had violated her covenant with God. God told Joshua He would not be with him anymore unless he destroyed whatever was devoted to destruction.

Joshua called Achan to come forward and said, "Waz up?" Achan replied, "It's true! I have sinned against the Lord. This is what I have done: I saw . . . I coveted . . . I took . . . I hid." There you have it—the *cycle of sin.*

The story is told of a little boy who was fishing. He was catching fish and having the time of his life. Every time he threw his line into the water he caught a fish. Early that morning, while digging for bait, he dug up what he thought were worms, but in reality were baby rattlesnakes. Time after time, as he reached into the bucket for more bait, the baby rattlesnakes would bite him. He would wince in pain, but he was having so much fun he kept right on fishing. Unfortunately, in the midst of having fun, the boy died without knowing what killed him.

That's the way it is when we mess with sin. The Bible says sin is pleasurable for a season, but in the final analysis it will destroy you. Today, if you are enslaved to sin, it's time to stand in front of the mirror and ask for forgiveness. The cycle of sin is easy to identify, and the only known cure is the blood of Jesus Christ. Break the power of sin by asking the Holy Spirit to fill you completely.

Memorize: 1 John 1:9

Prayer: Jesus, I know You died for my sin. Thanks not only for forgiving me of my sin, but for breaking the power of sin in my life.

Don't Worry—Be Happy

READ: Phil. 4:4-6

Everything must have been peachy in Philippi for Paul. If you scan the Book of Philippians you will find that Paul is always saying "Don't worry—be happy." The message is clear to all who read his letter. "Celebrate God all day, every day. I mean *revel* in Him." It must have been an absolute paradise for Paul. Nothing had to be going wrong for Paul as He penned this letter to His friends in Philippi.

But, *not everything* was right. As he wrote to his friends, he was chained up in a jail. What made the matter even worse was that something terrible was going on outside the prison. Men with impure motives were preaching Christ and taking offerings—not to advance the kingdom of God but to fill their own pockets.

Paul really had no reason to be happy. I wouldn't be happy if I was locked up in some grungy hole. Paul had no reason to rejoice—at least not about being in prison or about evil men. But He still had one thing to rejoice about. Phil. 1:18 says: "But what does it matter? The thing I rejoice in is the fact that no matter what kind of motive is represented, Christ is lifted up."

There's a lesson to be learned. Paul placed his circumstances in the context of God's overall activity in the world. Even though not everything was going as he planned, he was still able to rejoice over the things in his life that were advancing the kingdom of God.

Paul had the ability to look at things from God's perspective. He penned these words to the church at Corinth: We've been surrounded and battered by troubles, but we're not demoralized; we're not sure what to do, but we know God knows what to do. We've been tempted, but God has not left our side for one minute; we've been down, but we're getting back up (2 Cor. 1:8-10).

I realize we live in a world full of sin and evil. Not everything turns out the way we think it should. We have problems for which we don't seem to have solutions. If you're seeking to become *authentically His,* you will look through all the pain and find something to rejoice about.

Why? Because "we know that the one who raised the Lord Jesus from the dead will also raise us with Jesus and present us with you in his presence" (2 Cor. 4:14, NIV).

Memorize: 2 Cor. 4:8-10

Prayer: Jesus, You came into this world to give me abundant life. Help me find joy in life's journey.

Rules for Dating

READ: Rom. 8:1-9

A popular idea today that the media is trying to jam down our throats is that teens won't listen to the abstinence message. They say things like, "You're wasting your breath if you're going to try to sell young people on the notion they can say no to premarital sex." It's as if they believe you're incapable of understanding the Word of God and that it's not in your best interests to save yourself until marriage.

Surveys tell us that a significant percentage of high school females under the age of 18 are virgins. Although the percentage rate is lower among males, it still communicates *not everybody* is doing it. Who says you won't listen to this time-honored, biblically based message? Even young people who are sexually active are choosing to stop. This is called secondary virginity—a good concept that conveys the idea that you can start over again.

Peer pressure is the number one factor in influencing young people to give up and give in to premarital sex. The source of your security is found in your acceptance by others—especially your peers. Many times your self-worth and self-esteem are grounded in what others think about you.

God is looking for young people who understand their own unique-ness and are able to stand on the precepts and principles of the Word of God. He's looking for you to *lead the way* in sexual purity. To do this, you must begin now to set boundaries that will protect and provide for you.

Here is my set of rules that will guide you in your relationship with the opposite sex. These rules are guaranteed (if you follow them) to take you to your wedding night a virgin. Here we go:

1. Always date a person of like faith.
2. Remember: dating is no place for evangelism.
3. No prolonged kissing.
4. Hands always above the waist.
5. No hands under clothing.
6. Never remove any clothing.
7. Never lie down.

Don't forget—lead the way in sexual purity.

Memorize: Rom. 8:1-2

Prayer: Jesus, I live in a world that screams at me every day to let down my guard and give in to peer pressure. Thanks for living inside me and giving me power to overcome.

Spend Time in Authentic Relationship

READ: John 14:1

I am often asked, "How can I keep from failing in my relationship with God?" It's a searching question, and I have a sure-fire way to develop an intimate, personal, dynamic relationship with God. The Bible calls it "abiding in Christ."

What does the word *abide* mean? It indicates a permanence of position—a continuing commitment—not "I'll try God this week, and if He comes through for me I'll think about taking the next step." No, there is permanence in this word *abide*.

Let me share with you two key ingredients for abiding in Christ:

Spend Time in God's Word

If we want to abide in Christ, we must spend time in God's Word. We move at supersonic speeds in our daily agendas, and it becomes easy to transfer this attitude over into our relationship with God. Appetite is the issue here. If I have an appetite, I know my body is functioning normally. If I don't have an appetite, I have a clue something is wrong. It's the same way in my relationship with God. If I'm hungry for the Word, I know my relationship is healthy. If I have no appetite for the Word, that usually means something is not quite right in my relationship.

I read a great statement about the Word: "It's not enough to go through the word of God; the word of God must go through you."

Spend Time in Prayer

Second, if we are to abide in Christ, we must spend time in prayer. We can pray anytime, anywhere—even in school. You see, when we spend time in prayer, we begin to grow in intimate relationship with Him.

Your prayers don't have to be elegant; they have only to be sincere. Luke 18:13 gives us a great example of sincere prayer: "God be merciful to me a sinner" (KJV). That's what I call sincere.

How do you become authentically His? Abide permanently in Christ as He abides permanently in you.

Memorize: John 14:1

Prayer: Jesus, I want to abide in You. I thank You for Your permanence in my life. Teach me to spend time in Your Word, and teach me to pray.

Worship: You Must Be Present to Win

READ: John 4:21-26

I've discovered some pretty good definitions of worship, and I thought today would be a good day to share them with you. After all, you are going to church today. I remember going to some pretty dull services while I was growing up. I always blamed it on the song leader or the preacher. I became, at times, like the spiritual porker who always said: "Feed me. Feed me." Not any more—I've discovered that in worship *you must be present to win.*

Here are some great definitions of worship:

Worship happens when I realize that what I have been given is far greater than what I could ever give.

Worship happens when I realize that if it were not for His touch, I would still be hobbling and hurting, bitter and broken.

Worship is the half-glazed expression on the parched face of a desert pilgrim who has discovered that the oasis is not a mirage.

Worship is the thank-you that refuses to be silenced.

Worship is the lens through which I have a clear picture of God.

Worship is a human response to a divine revelation.

One of the most fascinating and challenging conversations of Jesus in His earthly ministry occurred at a well with a ragtag Samaritan woman. Ultimately, the conversation turned to the worship of God. That conversation with the woman brought forth Jesus' most important statement on what true worship is. There is no vagueness in His words nor confusion in His verbiage. Jesus gives a clear, decisive word on the real essentials of worship.

He said, "True worshipers will worship the Father in spirit and truth." Jesus clearly places the Father as the benchmark of true worship. Everything you do in worship must measure up with this mark of the Father. Jesus went on to say that the *attitude* of the heart and the *desire* of His Spirit are the things that make worship come alive.

If I go a day without expressing gratitude to the One who saved me, it would be well for me to remember once again what He has done for me.

Memorize: John 4:23-24

Prayer: Jesus, I want to magnify Your name today. Help me not to be distracted by anyone or anything as I worship You.

Virtual Reality

READ: Eph. 4:1-5

There's a new game sweeping across America. You'll find it in shopping malls, game rooms, and amusement parks. It's a fascinating five-minute trip into the world of 3-D. In the same malls there are posters that boast of 3-D designs. To tell the truth, I love to spend incredible amounts of time staring at these 3-D posters, trying to figure out what design is hidden within them.

My friend, Mike Boswith, introduced me to these posters, and now I'm an addict. I had one problem in the beginning: it all looked like confusion to me. Mike would stand in front of the poster and say things like "I can't believe you can't see those figures. Up in the corner you'll see a cross . . . there's a cone in the middle and a spiral at the side." I looked, and all I could see was confusion. He finally said, "Jim, here's what you have to do. You have to stand in front of the poster like you're standing in front of the mirror—relax your eyes and look past the picture into your reflection."

I did exactly what Mike said. Suddenly, what looked like confusion started taking shape, and I could see every figure perfectly. It took me three days, but I finally got the hang of it.

Many times our lives take shape the same way. Confusion sets in and we become lost. But I'm glad I had a voice giving me instructions. If your life is filled with confusion, do what I did:

I listened to someone who had mastered the art.

I looked past all the confusion.

I relaxed, and suddenly everything came into focus.

Nowadays it's easy for me to find focus. I practice every chance I get. I'm learning that if I want to make it through the confusing maze of this world and run on the road God wants me to travel, I must listen to His voice and look to the horizon—and there He is. In clear focus, I see the image of the one who has called me to lead the way.

Memorize: Eph. 4:1

Prayer: Jesus, help me to keep focused on You. Help me to look to You, the Perfecter of my faith.

Marathons and Marcus TUESDAY • 9

READ: Phil. 3:12-14

It was a hot, sultry day as I prepared to run my first marathon. Four months earlier I had blurted out something almost unconsciously as our local NYI council met to discuss how we could raise money for that year's missions project. There were all kinds of suggestions rolling around on the table—things like rock-a-thons, bike-a-thons, jump-a-thons, walk-a-thons, eat-a-thons, and—would you believe it?—sleep-a-thons! All of a sudden, I heard myself blurt out the words, "Why don't I run a marathon?"

Not wanting to run it alone, I invited my good friend Marcus to run with me. He said he would, and on July 4, 1993, Marcus and I were ready to go. The gun went off, and we began the run for missions. It was easy going the first 10 miles or so as we concentrated on finishing the race. Every once in a while, Marcus would look at me and say, "Why did I let you talk me into this?"

They told me that somewhere in the race we would "hit the wall." For me, that came at about 13 miles. I remembered what those who had run before me said, "When you hit the wall, keep on running. If you do, sooner or later you will break through and be able to finish." Determined not to quit, I kept on running.

We had run through the wall and were feeling fine when all of a sudden, at 20 miles, my knee gave out. In great pain I limped along, not knowing if I could keep on going. I stopped and allowed my friend, Jerry, to wrap my knee with a bandage.

My legs were stiff, and I was ready to give up. About that time, Marcus said to me: "We're going to finish this race together," and for seven miles, with his help, I was able to finish the only marathon I have ever run. As I crossed the finish line, the Lord began to teach me a lesson about leading the way. He said, "As you run the race I've marked out for you, don't ever forget—there is a Marcus in your life whom I have placed there to help you finish when you think you can't."

I thank God for a friend named Marcus. Without him I would have quit the race.

Memorize: Phil. 3:12-14

Prayer: Jesus, You have called me to lead the way. Sometimes that means I don't run out in front, but with those who need my encouragement to finish the race.

17

Love Letter from Heaven

READ: John 3:16

Falling in love is a beautiful thing! There are so many ways we can express love to that special person. I remember my first crush. I was about 11 years old, and I fell head over heels for an older girl named Gezelle. She was one of my sister's best friends, who often came over to the house. I don't think Gezelle ever knew I had a crush on her, but secretly I was in love.

Over the years I have learned there are three basic ways to communicate love. The first way really applies to the girls. They love to talk on the phone. It's so bad that I saw a girl the other day with a phone stuck in her ear. They talk about all kinds of things on the phone, but the major topic is guys. Guys have a very difficult time on the phone asking girls out. One was so nervous that, when he finally called the girl, he said, "Hello, this is concert and I'm wondering if you would like to go to the John with me . . . I mean, this is John . . ."

Another way we express love is by sending flowers. It's a great way to let someone know you really care. But the greatest way we express love is by writing love letters. They're full of ooey, gooey, mushy words you would say only to the one you love.

I've discovered the greatest love letter of all was written not by man, but by God. If you want to read the most intimate, dynamic, personal love letter, pick up the Word of God.

In reading this intimate letter, I've found that God is committed to three things.

1. He's committed to loving us. The Bible declares that "God demonstrated His love toward us in that while we were yet enemies against God, Christ died for us" (Rom. 5:8).
2. He's committed to loving us for eternity. We don't serve some fickle God who loves us only when we're good. We serve a God who laid down His life and went all the way to hell and back to demonstrate His love.
3. He's committed to our obeying Him. John 14:15 says: "If you love me you will obey my commands."

Read His Word today as a love letter from heaven.

Memorize: John 14:15

Prayer: Jesus, thank You for Your love letter. Help me today to demonstrate my love for You by living my life in radical obedience to Your Word.

Falling in Love with God THURSDAY · 11

READ: Eph. 5:1-2

We have discovered that God is madly in love with us. Do you want to know how you can fall madly in love with God? Obey your parents! That's right—you read it right—obey your parents!

You see, there is a dynamic tension in your home that could be causing friction. Your parents want to give you responsibility without authority, and you want authority without responsibility.

I discovered it all too well in my home. I have always had a great relationship with my dad, except for my senior year in high school. Something happened that year I wish had never happened. My dad and I were arguing one day about some work in the home. It was one of those stupid arguments that should never have taken place. My dad said one thing, and I countered with another. The house was getting hot—and it wasn't because it was 100 degrees outside. Both of us were at the boiling point when my dad said, "Jim, you're lazy!"

I was far from being lazy, and I began to tell him how much I worked for him around the church and home. I said, "Who mows the church lawn and our lawn for free? Who cleans the church for free? Who runs the bus route and helps you with evangelism? Who does his fair share around the house? If I'm anything, I'm certainly not lazy!" Neither of us could take it any more. The fight had begun, and for the first time in my life, I raised my hand against my father.

By the time it was over and my brothers were pulling me off of him, I had dealt a damaging blow to my father. It wasn't the punches I threw; it was my rebellion and lack of obedience that devastated my dad.

Sometimes we respond that way to our Heavenly Father. We throw punches of rebellion and disobedience that cut to the very heart of God. And just as I went to my earthly father and said, "I'm sorry," I can also go to my Heavenly Father and tell Him "I'm sorry" and through obedience show Him I love Him.

It's true! If I can't honor and obey my earthly father, how can I honor and obey my Heavenly Father? Fall in love with God—honor and obey your earthly parents. This in turn will bring honor to God.

Memorize: Eph. 5:1-2

Prayer: Jesus, thank You for giving me my parents. Even though we disagree at times, help me to honor You by honoring and obeying them.

The Big "D"—Debauchery

READ: Gal. 5:19-20

The devastation was horrendous. In the summer of 1993 the Midwest experienced some of the most devastating flooding in history. For weeks the water was relentless. The Mississippi River and other waterways flooded their banks, decimating the old boundaries. Destruction was unmistakable!

During the height of this disaster I flew over St. Louis, where the flood damage had literally shut down much of the city. You could not tell where the river's banks started or stopped. As I viewed this uncontrollable river, I began to think about the devastation sin can bring into our lives. Sexual sin in particular can be one of the most devastating sins to a young person.

There's a word in the Bible that relates to what I saw in the summer of 1993: *debauchery*. The word means stirring up emotions within you or your partner that cannot be satisfied within God's loving, logical limits. If you engaged in debauchery, you can be described as *one who has no boundaries.*

God has given us loving, logical limits to protect us and provide for us. Sometimes we think God is a cosmic cop standing at the very center of our lives, looking for ways to keep us from having too much fun—especially when it comes to relating to the opposite sex. Not true! God does not want to spoil your fun. He wants to give you life more abundantly. That means He wants you to experience a full and happy life without botching it up with the scars of sin.

In order for you to experience life to its fullest, God has placed some boundaries in your life. A boundary is a limiting, dividing line or mark. As a young person committed to leading the way in sexual purity, you have to set boundaries in your life that you will not cross—boundaries based upon the Word of God.

Young people frequently ask me, "How far is too far?" My answer is always the same: When you begin to stir up desires in you or your partner that cannot be satisfied within God's loving, logical limits, you've gone too far. Don't fall for "The Big Lie." Satan has one thing on his mind—he hates your guts and he wants to destroy you.

Memorize: John 10:10

Prayer: Jesus, I realize You have placed boundaries in my life to protect me. Empower me to lead the way in sexual purity.

Giving Little Things to a Big God

READ: Mark 11:1-3

I don't know about you, but there are some questions I'm going to ask God when I see Him. There are some statements made in the Word of God that just need more explanation. For instance, there is a statement Jesus made that I have been pondering over for a few days now . . .

"If anyone asks you why you are taking the donkeys, say that the master needs them, and he will send them at once."

Of course, I don't know who "he" was or what he looked like, but I do know what he gave. From the outset, one would think this was a very insignificant gift—but in fact, it was just the opposite. He gave Jesus a donkey on the Sunday He entered Jerusalem. We know it as Palm Sunday.

My question is simple: How did this man know the Lord needed the donkeys? Did Jesus stop by for a Coke and tell him He was going to send someone back to pick them up? Did this man have a vision? How did he know the Master needed this seemingly insignificant gift? Or is a gift *ever* insignificant?

I have a thought that continually runs through my mind: All of us have a donkey. We each have something in our lives that, if given back to God, could quite possibly advance the kingdom of God. Maybe you can sing or speak a word of encouragement or mow a shut-in's lawn. Perhaps you can start a Bible study in your school. Whatever you can do, that's your donkey. Just remember—your donkey belongs to Him. It really does, you know! The donkey was His and your gifts are His. How do I know that? The Greek says it this way: *If anyone asks you why you are taking the donkeys, you are to say, "Its Lord is in need."*

Jesus was using royal language. It's language that required a citizen to render to the king any item or service he or one of his emissaries might request. In making such a request, Jesus was claiming to be King.

Could it be that God wants to use your donkey and ride into another city, another nation, or even another heart? Will you let Him? Or will you hesitate? The guy with the donkey is just one in a long line of people—ordinary people like you—who gave little things to a big God.

God has quite a gallery of donkey givers. I wonder—are you included in that gallery?

Memorize: Eph. 5:1-2

Prayer: Jesus, help me to realize that You have gifted me with special abilities and talents to advance Your kingdom.

21

To Sum It All Up

READ: Prov. 3:5-6

I do something strange at the end of every year. It's a practice I have developed over a period of time. Every year I stand in front of the mirror of my life and evaluate the principles that have helped me lead the way. This ritual has a way of helping me chart my new course and reminds me where I am going.

Many young people approach life like a jellyfish. They just go with the flow and allow the tide of popularity to wash them in and out. Of course, if we are Christian we know this is not how we are to approach life. God has redeemed us that we might go against the current of destructive thinking.

God has called you to lead the way as a prayer warrior. He has called you to win your friends to Christ. He calls you to sexual purity. Finally, He calls you to lead the way by serving your neighbor.

Because He called me, I continue to cultivate a list of immovable truths that help me define the course God wants me to take. They are brilliant beams of light that guide me as I maneuver through the currents of life. Here are some of the highlights:

- Integrity is how I live when no one is watching.
- Pray more—worry less.
- Success begins with a pure heart.
- Listen more—speak less.
- Never let the urgent crowd out the important.
- When you can't trace God's hand, trust His heart.
- God has forgiven me; I should do the same.
- Don't put off till tomorrow what I can do today.
- Apprehend the attitude of gratitude daily.
- Love God. Love life. Love yourself. Love others.
- Be a promise keeper—go against the flow.

To sum it all up: approach life like a mountain expedition. Enjoy the majestic view. Explore uncharted territory. Make friends with the Guide. Count on your team members and your equipment. Enjoy the cool mountain streams. Then, when the journey is finished, enjoy your new home. Bask in the light of His grace. Warm yourself in the glowing radiance of His love.

Memorize: Prov. 3:5-6

Prayer: Jesus, help me live my life on the principles of Your Word.

Building Castles in the Sand

READ: Matt. 7:24-27

I remember growing up in San Diego, where going to the beach was a common activity for my family. We loved to go to the beach so we could try out our cool vocabulary—words like "Dude!" "Groovy!" "Far out!" As a kid, I always enjoyed body surfing, throwing Frisbees, and wrapping seaweed around my sister's legs. But there was one thing I thought was very strange: People would spend all day in the sand building sand castles. I admit—I have seen some really elaborate sand castles in my day, but I never had time to build one. There were always too many other things I wanted to do.

Even as a young person, I knew that at the end of the day, when the tide rolled in, those castles built by human hands would slowly erode away, and soon it would be as though they had never existed.

It's funny how the lessons I understood as a young man are still pictured on the screen of my mind. I realized that the castles made of sand would be washed away before sunset. And no matter how hard we try to keep the waves from crashing against our best efforts, we can never stop the inevitable.

Life has an unusual way of teaching us about the eternal. Young people are trying to build castles they think will stand—yet no matter how determined and diligent they work, the tide still rises and the end comes. It's only those castles built on the Rock, Jesus Christ, that will stand.

Wise is the teen who does not treat this world like a permanent home. Many today live as if the world will last forever. They're wrong!—we are all in transit. One day we will have to disembark this world, and wise is the teen who is ready when the Father says, "Come on home."

I'm glad I decided at a very young age to build my life on the Rock, Jesus Christ. It has kept me from building castles in the sand, which are here today and gone tomorrow.

Memorize: Matt. 7:25

Prayer: Jesus, I want my life to be built upon a Rock-solid foundation. Your Word is my foundation. May it guide every decision I make, and may my life always glorify You.

Rough Hands, Callused Hearts

READ: Rev. 3:20

I've had them all my life! Well—a good part of my life. They are called calluses: layer upon layer of nerveless skin that has been created over time. They tell me calluses are the body's defense against hours upon hours of gripping and squeezing. I know it all too well. Through my teenage years and beyond, it seems I was always digging, building, or roofing. At first my hands were very tender and soft. I constantly had blisters that would crack and bleed. But over time my hands became rough.

I was always aware of the calluses on my hands, but it was difficult at times to see the calluses that exist elsewhere—those found not on the hand, but on the heart. How does this happen?—by being hearers, but not doers, of the Word.

The hardened heart—you remember the story about the landowner. He had leased his vineyard to some men, and when it came time for the harvest he sent his servants to receive his share of the take. Heartbreak came as one by one the workers were beaten, murdered, and stoned. What would you do? I know what I would have done: I would have gotten a clue and quit sending servants. Then I would have done what any law-abiding citizen would do—call the cops. No doubt that is what the landowner did? I don't think so. If you are familiar with the story, you know that he kept on sending his servants—and finally his son.

I can't believe this end to the story. Yet on the landscape of our lives, Jesus wanted to demonstrate a God who is committed to redeeming us. No price was too high, no distance too far. God was determined to find us and to save us. His greatest creation was His plan to redeem you and me. Hey—it's the story of the gospel: Jesus was pierced for our transgressions so that He might slash through the calluses of our heart. Why is He so patient with us? I'll tell you why—He wants to redeem us.

God comes to your house, walks to the door of your heart, and knocks. He waits patiently until you open the door. And, you know, it's up to you to open the door. It's an important step in becoming *authentically His*.

Memorize: Rev. 3:20

Prayer: Jesus, help me to be not only a hearer of Your Word but a doer of Your Word as well. May my heart always be tender to Your Spirit.

Betrayed by a Friend WEDNESDAY • 17

READ: Matt. 26:50

Betrayed! That's an interesting word. Author Max Lucado says the word *betrayed* is a weapon found only in the hands of one you love. Those who dislike you—those who perhaps hate you—have no such weapon. They couldn't—for the very heart of the word *betrayed* depicts an intimate relationship. Only our friends or the ones we love can betray us.

Perhaps you have known the sting of betrayal. You have been wounded by words that cut like a knife. Betrayal goes something like this: "I don't love you anymore!" "I love you, but your mother and I can't live together anymore . . . we just don't love each other!" "I know I promised to go on that trip with you, but I have so many other things I really need to take care of!" "I know I said I would keep that confidential; it just slipped out!" Betrayal never comes from an enemy, only from a friend. You can sum up the word *betrayal* in a few short words: *when your world turns against you.*

When betrayal comes your way, how will you respond? Jesus handled it in a most unusual way. Let's take a look.

When Jesus saw Judas, He said, "Friend!" Hey, if it were me, I would have used some other choice words, like "traitor," "coward," and "spineless jellyfish." Jesus used the word "friend," and that is significant. Jesus saw things we could never see. Jesus knew Judas had been led astray by Satan himself. He knew how hard it was for Judas to do the right thing. He didn't condone what Judas was doing, but He did try to understand.

If you want to understand Jesus, look where He looked. Jesus looked to the horizon. When He was betrayed, He fixed His eyes on home. The best way to keep your balance when a friend betrays you is to keep your eyes fixed on the Author and Perfecter of your faith.

Just as the Father was committed to His Son, He is also committed to you. So when you feel betrayed, when you feel the sting of the betrayer's kiss, just remember the words of Jesus: "I will never leave you or forsake you" (Heb. 13:5).

When you feel that everyone and everything has turned against you, remember: all of heaven's army is turned toward you. That will bring you strength.

Memorize: Heb. 13:5

Prayer: Jesus, betrayal is such an ugly thing. Help me show compassion and love to those who feel betrayed.

It Ain't Over Till the Fat Lady Sings

READ: Eph. 1:5-6

Every Monday night for over a decade I heard these words reverberate from my television: "TURN OUT THE LIGHTS—THE PARTY'S OVER." Don Meredith sang this song to remind a national football audience that a thumping was on the horizon.

However, there were those who didn't take too kindly to Don's limited repertoire. The response was overwhelming: every Monday night during football season, you would see a sign that demonstrated the attitude of these dyed-in-the-wool fans. Offering words of hope for their favorite team, these fans would splash paint on a king-size bed sheet for all the world to read: "It Ain't Over Till the Fat Lady Sings!"

It's easy to jump to conclusions, isn't it? We worry over the most insignificant things. Yet it is always good for us to be reminded that God is still in control of our lives.

It's true! There have been times we have jumped to conclusions, only to be surprised by a strange curve thrown our way. Come to think of it, God is good at that. You remember some of these specific times, don't you?

Remember when a teenager, armed with only a slingshot and a stone, beat the giant who was over nine feet tall? Nobody would ever have dreamed of cheering for the underdog. But God did!

Remember those three Hebrew teenagers who were thrown into the fiery furnace? No one gave them any hope of coming out alive. But God had other plans!

Remember the dead-end street that led to Golgotha and the tomb? Three days later, all you had was an empty tomb.

What about that army of teenagers who have determined to lead the way? God will use them to turn the world upside down.

When you face circumstances that spell "The End," remember—God is intimately involved in your life. Never assume that the end is inevitable. In God's performances, the lights are always burning, the party is always beginning, and *life ain't over till God gives the final Amen!*

Memorize: Eph. 1:5-6

Prayer: Jesus, when my hour seems the darkest, may Your light break in and bring me hope and peace.

Sex Is Not a Four-letter Word

READ: Gen. 1:27-28

Dana Carvey of "Saturday Night Live" fame portrays a character you might recognize. She is called the "Church Lady," a prudish old woman in a long dress down to her ankles and her hair pulled back in a bun. She says things like: "Welllll, isn't that special?" and "I wonder who made you do that—could it be . . . Satan?" The Church Lady pokes fun at Christianity, but one of her passions is sex. Carvey characterizes the view that Christians consider sex a four-letter word. There are many others today who are trying to convince us that God is a God who condemns sex and sexuality.

Sex is not a four-letter word or a dirty word. It's not wrong or shameful, nor is it sinful. As a matter of fact, it was God who thought up sex in the first place. Just look at all the things God thought up—He created hair, skin, eyebrows, eyes, eyelashes, noses, mouths, necks, arms, fingers, breasts (yes, you read that right), belly buttons (I'm making you nervous now!), reproductive organs, legs—the list could go on and on. In other words, it was God who created you.

Sex has been part of God's plan from the very beginning. When God told man and woman, "Be fruitful, and multiply" (Gen. 1:28, KJV), He was saying *Obey Me by participating in sexual activity.* Just look through the Word of God, and you will find some pretty open accounts of sexual encounters. Read the Song of Solomon, and you will discover some language that would make the Church Lady's hair stand on end.

But—the scripture is very clear about the fact that sex outside of marriage is wrong. The writer of Hebrews says: "And the marriage bed shall be kept pure, for God will judge the adulterer and all the sexually immoral" (Heb. 13:4).

God created sex. God intended it to be a very fulfilling and exciting experience between men and women who have committed themselves to each other through the act of marriage. He wants to protect you and provide for you an atmosphere of trust. Trust is the glue that fulfills marriage. God wants to protect your virginity, because on your wedding night virginity is the greatest gift you could ever give to that special person. I challenge you to lead the way in sexual purity.

Memorize: 1 Cor. 6:15-17

Prayer: Jesus, I realize You want to protect me and provide for me. Help me stand upon Your Word when the world says "Just do it."

Invitations

READ: Luke 9:23-26

I love to receive invitations, especially the ones that involve food—those are my favorite. That's why I included that kind of invitation in my marriage proposal.

It was a beautiful Arkansas evening, and my wife-to-be, Cindi, and I were all alone. I had been contemplating for weeks how I was going to pop the question. I didn't know what kind of response I was going to receive from my "Miss Arkansas." The time came, and the hour was getting late. Butterflies were fluttering in the pit of my stomach as I mustered enough courage to ask the question. I began my introductory remarks with: "I was wondering if you would like to share my grocery bill with me for the rest of our lives." Wham! The question was out before I knew it, and the response was just as quick: "Yes, I would love to be Mrs. James N. Williams."

Invitations are wonderful. They may be words written on cards or received by phone. Whatever the method, when you get one, it means you are to be honored.

You know, I have discovered that the most incredible invitations are not found in letters or by a phone call—they are found in the Word of God. You can't read the Word of God without finding invitation after invitation.

Hey—the God I serve is a God of invitations. He extends them every day to young people just like you. I need to remind you that His invitation is not just for sharing groceries—it is for a lifetime. It's an invitation that calls you to come and follow Him. He's calling you to take up residence in His world, not yours.

Anyone who is thirsty, hungry, or lonely can find rest. Yet the greatest invitation of all is for anyone who needs forgiveness. It is universal and is signed in crimson by His Son, Jesus Christ.

What are you doing today with God's invitation? What are you doing with His intimate request to live with Him for eternity? If you boil everything down to its purest level, His invitation is the only one that really counts.

Memorize: Luke 9:23-24

Prayer: Jesus, thank You for the invitation to follow You. Help me to take up my cross daily.

Worry: The Thing Everyone Likes to Do!

READ: Phil. 4:6

Have you been caught worrying lately? I mean one of those old-fashioned, good-for-nothing, caught-in-a-corner bouts with worry! You know the kind I'm talking about. All young people experience worry over something at some time in their lives—things like:

1. Whether your face is going to look smooth as silk or like Crater Valley on your first date.
2. Whether that jelly roll you just ate will look good on you—if you know what I mean.
3. Whether that speck in your mouth is a cavity—or the meat that got stuck in your teeth during dinner.
4. Whether your braces will get caught in your significant other's braces and the only way you can separate them is to ask your potential father-in-law to pry them apart.

Oh, I almost forgot! You have also told me you worry about whether your mom and dad are going to stay together. You said you're worried about the future and what it will hold for you. You're worried about AIDS. I even heard you're worried about how you, as a committee of one, can have a significant impact on your world.

I must confess to you that even I worry on occasion, and when I worry I'm good at it. I worry about my dog and what he thinks of me when I'm just stepping out of the shower. I worry about things getting caught in my mustache while I'm eating and no one will be kind enough to tell me that my worry has become a reality. I worry about dietitians discovering that Jell-O and cottage cheese were fattening all along.

You know, worry tends to make us forget who is in charge. It brings clouds of confusion into our lives until we can't see the sunlight of His sovereignty. Satan knows this trick all too well. His distortion of perspective should always be guarded against.

The undeniable truth is this: when we begin to focus on ourselves, we begin to worry. The next time you begin to worry, remember—God is sovereign, and He is in control of your life.

Memorize: Phil. 4:6

Prayer: Jesus, help me not to focus on myself or my circumstances, but help me keep my eyes fixed on You.

I've Got Friends in High Places

READ: Heb. 7:22-28

Country musician Garth Brooks sings a popular song called "I've Got Friends in Low Places." He says he is going to kick on down to the Oasis (bar) because all his friends are in low places. I've been thinking about low living lately. Strange, I know, but it seems odd to me that young people would choose to walk the low road when we were *made for high places.*

I recently read a story told by Danish philosopher Søren Kierkegaard about some geese who landed in a farmer's backyard while on one of their annual treks. The farmer "adopted" them, caring for them and making sure they had plenty of grain to eat each day.

As time went on while living the easy life, the geese became fat and lazy and lost their desire to fly. When they heard the familiar honks of their flying friends, they would look up—and then go on about their business. Once in a while, one of them would feel a stirring deep within to soar again where the air was pure. When that urge became too strong, the goose would extend its wings and become airborne for a few seconds—only to drop to the ground like a rock a few feet away.

The easy, undisciplined life had taken its toll. After a while the geese completely lost the urge to soar to high places, and they no longer listened when their friends would fly over, honking their call to a higher, nobler life.

God created you for more than low living. Press on today with holy determination to a Christlike character. We can live in the swamp of self-centeredness, or we can reach for the high places of spiritual maturity.

By the way . . . I just want to remind you that you have *a Friend in high places.* As a matter of fact, He is calling you now to lead the way by walking the high road.

Memorize: Heb. 7:27

Prayer: Jesus, thanks for being my Friend in high places. Show me daily which road to travel, and help me not to be detoured on roads that lead nowhere.

The Vision Within

READ: Ps. 121

Have you ever been let down—blown away by unrealized expectations? We all know the sting of a close friend or family member who backed out of our life when we needed him or her the most. It has been said: "Anything less than God will let you down." If you take that a step further, you realize that anything not rooted in God will have no lasting value.

For every possible problem you face, God gives you corresponding grace. I guess you could say that for every need there is a supernatural resource. For every question there is an answer. For every problem there is a solution. If you are weak, He can make you strong. If you have been let down, He will lift you up.

If you understand this principle, you know it can change your life. Jeremiah understood it when he penned the words, "Ah Lord God! Behold, You have made the heavens and the earth by Your great power and by Your outstretched arm! Nothing is too difficult for You" (Jer. 32:17).

There are several ways God supports and strengthens you when you feel someone has let you down:

1. His Word—which communicates to us that we are truly significant.
2. Prayer—Ps. 25 reminds us that even though we choose to walk the right path, it will not always be easy. Therefore, we must know where to look for help.
3. The Holy Spirit—who gives us power to overcome every circumstance of life.

As you allow God to do great things for you, even in less than the best circumstances, He will give you inner strength to go beyond yourself. God will begin to develop the *vision within* as you experience His power through the Holy Spirit.

Remember:

If you want to be distressed—look within.
If you want to be defeated—look back.
If you want to be distracted—look around.
If you want to be dismayed—look ahead.
If you want to be delivered—look up.

Memorize: Ps. 121:1-4

Prayer: Jesus, I know You have a vision for my life. Help me to discover every day Your plan for my life.

Can Jesus Trust You?

READ: John 19:25-27

It must have been a most extraordinary thing to be called "the disciple whom Jesus loved." I guess you could say that John was Jesus' best friend. To be Jesus' best friend meant that Jesus trusted him . . . with writing His Gospel . . . with His mother . . . and with His love.

To be Jesus' best friend smacks of something inappropriate. But the fact is, that's what the relationship between Jesus and John was. It indicates that Jesus has some whom He counts as better friends than others.

I wonder what would happen if you were identified in all of Christianity as Jesus' best friend. You would be on the cover of every magazine in the world. What do you think it would do to you? Do you think it would change your life? Would you write a book or cut a CD or go on the road doing "Best Friend of Jesus" seminars? And yet, didn't Jesus have as much right as any of us to have a best friend? If so, wasn't it critically important that He choose someone He could trust to be His best friend, with the confidence that that person would never misuse their relationship?

You have probably been asked many times, "Do you trust Jesus?" I hope the answer has been a resounding "Yes! I trust Him completely!" But let me ask just once: "Does Jesus trust *you?*" Can He trust you to meet His needs, to fulfill His mission, to be what He's called you to be?

The world today needs young people who will become *authentically His.* I may have a skewed perception of reality, but it appears to me that there is a long list of young people who will lead the way in success, but a rather short list of young people who will lead the way in less than the best conditions.

Can Jesus trust you? Ten thousand times you might be asked, "Do you trust Jesus?" but perhaps today you can say, "Jesus, You can trust *me!*"

Memorize: Matt. 16:18

Prayer: Jesus, I have told You many times that I trust You. Today You can trust me as I say, "You can count on me."

Lead the Way by Winning
a Friend to Christ

READ: Prov. 17:17

Dr. Wilford Funk of Funk and Wagnalls was asked to go through his dictionary and come up with what he considered to be the 10 most expressive words in the English language. Here are his results:

The most bitter word: *alone*

The most revered word: *mother*

The most tragic word: *death*

The most inspiring word: *faith*

The saddest word: *forgotten*

The most beautiful word: *love*

The cruelest word: *revenge*

The coldest word: *no*

The most peaceful word: *tranquillity*

He went on to say that the warmest word in the English language is *friend*. It's a fact of life: if you have one or two real friends in life—I'm talking about the type who will walk with you through the whole process of life itself—you would consider yourself fortunate.

I consider myself very fortunate to have friends who have stood by me even when I wasn't worth standing by. Larry Hess is that kind of friend to me. Larry and I have been friends for a very long time. He has been my supporter, my coworker, and my cheerleader. I love Larry and am glad he has always been my friend.

But the greatest blessing I have received in life came in the form of an invitation. This invitation was initiated by God, who said that I can be friends with Jesus.

Many people around you are seeking the kind of friendship I have just described. They want more than superficial relationships. They want someone to care for them and accept them just the way they are. Young people today are looking for friendship with God, and they have only one hope: you! They need to know what genuine friendship is, and God is depending on you to lead the way.

Memorize: Prov. 17:17

Prayer: Jesus, thanks for being a Friend who never leaves me. Help me be a friend who loves at all times.

33

Standing in the Gap

READ: Gen. 18:16-33

There are young people around you who have given in to the myth that they cannot stay sexually pure and have bought into the lie that "safe sex" is the only solution to their sexuality. Even our public officials and school administrators have given up on the fight for purity. They are passing out condoms to students, convincing themselves that this is the only reasonable choice left to make.

The safe-sex message perpetuates five dangerous ideas that will continue to destroy what is left of the moral fiber of your generation. The unintended consequences of "safe sex" are the belief in the following myths:

1. That "safe sex" is achievable.
2. That everyone is doing it.
3. That everyone expects young people to have sex.
4. That it's a good thing.
5. That their peers are educated in "safe sex."

Every one of these consequences leads to sexual promiscuity. But every generation has a remnant of young people who have been called out to stand in the gap for their peers. You are part of that remnant.

Bob Diehm wrote a song with you in mind, called "Standing in the Gap." Bob writes:

> *I love you, friend, more than I can say,*
> *And I know the life you've chosen holds you captive day by day.*
> *And I don't know, friend, if the message made it through,*
> *Of the Jesus I have told you of and the life He has for you.*
> *So, I'll keep on praying and I'll be there for you,*
> *'Til the Savior's love breaks through to you.**

Today more than ever, your friends need you to stand in the gap for them. Lead the way!

Memorize: John 17:20-21

Prayer: Jesus, thanks for standing in the gap for me when I was confused and lonely. Help me to stand in the gap and pray for my friends.

*"Standing in the Gap" © by Bob Diehm, The Diehm Project and Still Small Voice Music, 1993. Used with permission.

In Christ Alone

READ: Phil. 3:12-14

They say it was the greatest comeback in NFL playoff history. The Houston Oilers had dominated the Buffalo Bills for the first half and were leading 38-3. Early in the second half, quarterback Jim Kelly was injured, and for most of the fans all hope was gone. No one could bring the Bills back from that kind of deficit—no one except a backup quarterback named Frank Reich.

You see, it appeared no one remembered that during Frank's college days at Maryland he was in a similar situation and brought the Terrepins back from the same deficit. One player *did* remember, though, and right before Frank entered the game, he said to him, "Frank Reich, you did it once before—you can do it again." With that confidence, Frank entered the game and orchestrated the greatest comeback in NFL history.

After the game, the media thronged him and asked how he could perform on such a superhuman level. Frank looked at the sea of media types and quoted these words:

In Christ alone will I glory,
Though I could pride myself in battles won.
For I have been blessed beyond measure
And by His strength I have overcome.

In Christ alone I place my trust
And find my glory in the power of the Cross.
In every victory let it be said of me
*My source of strength, my source of hope is Christ alone.**

I hope your source of strength and source of hope is in Christ alone. Many times you will be tempted to put your faith and trust in your abilities, talents, or successes. Don't give in to that lie. The truth of the matter rests in your relationship with a loving Heavenly Father. He is your Source, and you stand today not by your strength, but by His grace.

Memorize: Phil. 1:9

Prayer: Jesus, I want to build my life on Your foundation. Help me today to demonstrate You in everything I say and do.

*"In Christ Alone," by Shawn Craig and Don Koch. Copyright © 1990 Paragon Music Corp./ASCAP. All rights reserved. Used with permission of Benson Music Group, Inc.

Dying to Lead the Way

READ: Gal. 2:20

Well, thanks for coming along on this journey with me. I hope you're serious about what it means to have an authentic relationship with an intimate, personal, loving Heavenly Father. If you're serious about leading the way, you're going to have to die! That's right—I said *die*. Writing to the church at Galatia, the apostle Paul said, "I've been crucified with Christ. I no longer live, but Christ lives within me" (Gal. 2:20).

Paul is writing about a long word that is difficult to understand at times. It's called sanctification. It means that I have become dead to sin and alive unto God. I no longer want sin to control my life; I want my life to be controlled by the Holy Spirit. Wouldn't it be great if your parents or pastor were to ask you, "What did you do this week?" and you responded, "Oh, I died!" "What?" "Yeah! I've been crucified with Christ! I'm dead. I'm history—I no longer live, but Christ lives within me!"

I've noticed young people treat their relationship with God as if they were on a spiritual roller coaster. One day they are up on the mountain, and the next day they are in the valley. They go to a church camp or retreat and have a spiritual "frozen moment." They come home, the emotion wears off, and they're right back doing the same things all over again. Nothing has changed. Young people, if we are called to lead the way, we must come to the point in our lives that we say no to sin and yes to God.

To say yes to God you must die to sin. This means you hold nothing back in your relationship with God. Remember: you're on a cross—you're dying—and there is no way you could ever hold anything in your hands. Your hands have been nailed to the Cross with Christ. Let me ask you a question: What are you holding back from God? Relationships, future, security? "God, I trust You with everything in my life, but I can't trust You with my relationships with the opposite sex." Hey, don't hold anything back from God. You can trust Him! You can trust Him to the point that you're *dying* to lead the way.

Memorize: Gal. 2:20

Prayer: Jesus, I hold nothing back from You today. I trust You with every area of my life and ask You to come alive in me as I die to sin.